7 Is My Favorite Number!
A Kwanzaa Celebration

Dedicated to My Ancestors...Ubuntu...

7 Is My Favorite Number!
A Kwanzaa Celebration

Copyright © 2022 by Dr. Talaya L. Tolefree
Written by Dr. Talaya L. Tolefree
Illustrated by Simbarashe Langton Vera

All rights reserved. No part of this book may be used or reproduced in any manner whatsoever without the prior written permission of the author.

On day **1** we celebrate **Umoja/Unity** in our community.

We light the **Black** candle to celebrate our Black skin and everything that makes us African.

On day 2 we light a **Red** candle to celebrate **Kujichagulia/Self-Determination**...

as we remember our ancestors' contributions to this nation!

On day 3 we light a Green candle to celebrate Ujima/Collective Work and Responsibility.

Traditional African Market Place  Black

On day 4 we light a Red candle to celebrate **Ujamaa/Cooperative Economics**. Our Elders tell us stories and show us important pictures from the past.

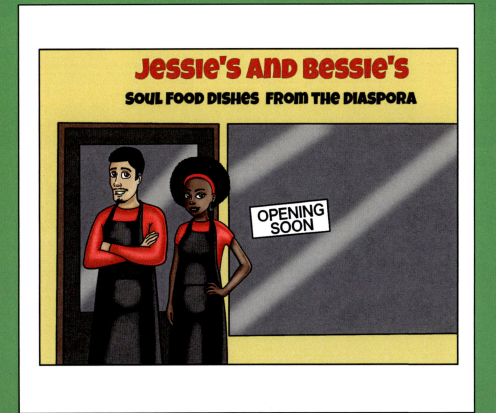

Wall Street Black Entrepreneurship

We begin to dream and create plans for
a future that will last.

On day 5 we light a Green candle to celebrate Nia/Purpose.

African Pyramids

Selma March

President Barack Obama and Family

Supreme Court Justice Ketanji Brown Jackson and Madam Vice President Kamala Harris

On day 7 we light the last Green candle to celebrate **Imani/Faith**. We listen to our community leaders share their reflections. We have fun as we make new connections.

Our Elders teach us the importance of having faith in ourselves, parents, and community, that's the way we spread Kwanzaa Unity.

Celebration

Sankofa is a Ghanaian word that means **looking back to move forward.** Let's take a Sankofa Moment back to the birth of Kwanzaa. Dr. Maulana Karenga, literally, embodied Sankofa when he created Kwanzaa in the 1960's during one of many times when Black people of African descent were collectively and explicitly resisting American apartheid. The search for liberation, identity and culture had been severely broken, due to centuries of racialized slavery that led to the eras of Reconstruction, Jim Crowism, the Civil Rights movement and to the current subjugation of Black people.

Dr. Maulana Karenga researched and experienced African culture and traditional practices to reconstruct Black culture and identity in the form of a seven-day celebration. The humanity, love, culture, values, brilliance, creativity, collectivism and resilience of the African Diaspora were highlighted. The Kwanzaa values and principles offer Black people and the world a comprehensive approach to understanding traditional African and African American values and belief systems.

In the 1990's I was gifted Kwanzaa ideologies and practices by Rev. Dr. Paulette Sankofa. She was the director of our community's cherished national afterschool program, Project SPIRIT (Strength, Perseverance, Imagination, Responsibility, Integrity and Talent), where Black children were taught to be proud of themselves, their culture and history using Kwanzaa as the foundation for their development.

My participation in Project Spirit started as a parent and site coordinator, then transitioning to Program Director as Dr. Sankofa moved on to another position. We continued to celebrate Kwanzaa in Project SPIRIT classrooms, community gatherings, and at home with close friends and family. Kwanzaa became deeply woven into the fabric of our lives.

Stemming from the past, the humanity and culture of Black people has been challenged and attacked through acts of violence and senseless fatalities. Much of my work focuses on relationship building, restoration and creating equitable experiences in schools and community. **"Kasserian Ingera"** or **"And how are the children?"** This is a traditional greeting from the African Masai Tribe. Many parents and educators are grappling with the question posed by this greeting. They recognize there are a limited number of children's books that represent and affirm Black children and their culture.

"7 Is My Favorite Number!" builds upon the foundation of Kwanzaa to affirm Black children. Historical and current achievements of Black people are embedded in this celebratory story of Kwanzaa and Black culture.

"Akwaaba" is a Ghanaian word that means welcome. You are welcome to join us in sharing the spirit of Kwanzaa to affirm and uplift Black children. We believe in **"Ubuntu"** an African word that means **"Humanity to others"** or "I am because we are." As human beings, we are all relatives and deserve to be celebrated, loved and treated with dignity and respect. We hope you enjoy our book as you find hidden treasures in the form of words, signs and symbols that give deep meaning and affirmation to Black children. Let us practice the Kwanzaa Principle **"Kuumba"** to leave our community better than we inherited it.

- Dr. Talaya L. Tolefree

Thank you for choosing our book!
If you enjoy our book,
please write a review to help reach more readers like you!

Made in the USA
Las Vegas, NV
30 April 2023